Original title:
The Roof of Tomorrow

Copyright © 2025 Creative Arts Management OÜ
All rights reserved.

Author: Micah Sterling
ISBN HARDBACK: 978-1-80587-211-5
ISBN PAPERBACK: 978-1-80587-681-6

## A Skylit Sanctuary

In a house full of beams,
Cats plot their grand schemes.
Under stars made of glass,
They imagine their class.

A parrot sings loud chords,
While the goldfish plays cards.
The fridge hums a sweet tune,
As the light sneaks by noon.

On the window, a crow,
Wears a hat made of snow.
Chasing shadows around,
They spin round and round.

With laughter in every crack,
Who knew walls could snack?
A sanctuary bright,
Full of funny delight!

## **Trails of Illumination**

Chasing beams like a light,
Socks dance in delight.
Lamps laugh with a flick,
As a toaster does a trick.

Bouncing off the walls,
A raccoon hears the calls.
Clouds of popcorn appear,
With flavors we hold dear.

Underneath the glow,
They plan their wild show.
Mice in hats make their way,
To join the fun today.

Where giggles fill the air,
And cake sits with flair.
Every trail lit bright,
Leads to pure delight!

## Beneath a Tapestry of Dreams

Under frayed, quilted strands,
Puppies play in bands.
They wear capes made of yarn,
And sing songs till dawn.

A dragon made of sweets,
Dances on tiny feet.
In this fantastical space,
Everyone knows their place.

With a bounce and a leap,
Kittens plot while they sleep.
Each cloud a soft pillow,
Squeaks of joy will follow.

In this land of delight,
Where nonsense feels right.
A sanctuary unique,
With a dash of mystique!

## Ascending Into New Beginnings

Up we rise, oh so high,
Chasing birds in the sky.
Every step a giggle,
With a playful wiggle.

A squirrel dons a cape,
Making superhero shapes.
With acorns as his props,
He never, ever stops.

Through the laughter we glide,
On a merry-go ride.
Jumping into the fray,
As we dance and play.

In this grand leap of fate,
We toast to our state.
With joy that won't end,
As we climb around the bend!

## Wings Beneath Endless Stars

In a night so vast and wide,
We wear pajamas as we glide.
With wings like bedsheets, we will soar,
Over trees, and maybe more!

Cacti wave and rooftops shake,
A waltz of squirrels, make no mistake.
Who knew the night had such a dance?
Look, the moon is in a prance!

## Shelter of Ambitions

Underneath this hodgepodge roof,
Dreams are made, goofballs in proof.
With paper planes and wild schemes,
We're launching laughter into beams.

A bird with glasses flies right by,
He quips, 'Don't let your dreams fly high!'
Yet up we float with foolish delight,
As marshmallows canvas the night.

## A New Dawn Beckons

Morning comes with a silly grin,
To wake the world and let laughs begin.
Toasters pop with bread awry,
Squeaking tea kettles laugh and sigh.

The sun peeks in, a mischievous spy,
Tickling trees while butterflies fly.
Pajama parties still in new light,
Sipping joy with giggles in sight.

## Ether's Embrace

In clouds so fluffy, we bump and soar,
Tickled by the giggles of galore.
A puppet show of shadows dance,
Ether whispers, 'Join the fancy prance!'

Stars in tutus, twirl and twist,
A comical sci-fi dream can't be missed.
With popcorn clouds as our tasty feast,
We laugh, we joke, a cosmic beast!

## **Where Dreams Touch the Clouds**

On rooftops high, we jump and play,
With laundry flying, come what may.
A pigeon steals my sandwich, bold,
  While I recount the tales of old.

Our diorama of a lively scene,
Where rooftops host a trampoline.
The sky is vast, as jokes take flight,
We bounce and laugh until the night.

## Echoes of an Evolving Skyline

We climbed upon that creaky ledge,
To check our hair against the hedge.
With mirrors up, we strike a pose,
As clouds critique our fashion woes.

The buildings wave like old friends greet,
While pigeons jest and dance on feet.
A skyline shifts, it's quite absurd,
As laughter echoes, truly heard.

## Tapestry of Tomorrow's Light

A patchwork quilt of tiles and dreams,
We weave our stories, bursting seams.
With cats that lounge and squirrels that plot,
While sunbeams share the tale they sought.

Roof parties host a grand charade,
As ice cream melts in sun's parade.
A funny hat, a comic dance,
We leap and giggle in a trance.

## Reflections on a Distant Firmament

Upon the roof, the stars align,
As we sip soda, feeling fine.
With dreams as big as moonlit pies,
We laugh with fireflies in disguise.

A telescope points at neighbors' woes,
As high-tech gnomes strike silly poses.
The cosmos chuckles at our spree,
With every whim, we fancy-free.

## **Moonlit Future Paths**

Under the glow of a silver beam,
We dance on dreams, or so it seems.
With giggles loud, we trip in time,
As socks and shoes become a rhyme.

Jumping puddles of wishful thought,
In silly hats, our minds are taught.
Future's a jester, laughing too,
With every step, we paint anew.

The moon winks down, a playful guide,
As we skip along this merry ride.
Today may frown, but wait and see,
Tomorrow's laughter sets us free.

In our heads, ideas collide,
Like bouncing balls, they giggle wide.
So here we go, a dance of fate,
With chuckles bright, we contemplate.

## A Dome of Endless Inspiration

Beneath a dome of colorful schemes,
We build our castles, we chase our dreams.
With crayons bright and paper thin,
We're architects of silly grin.

In this palace made of cheer,
There's always room for fun and beer.
Ideas bounce, they whirl and twirl,
With every challenge, our minds unfurl.

Colored windows let in a breeze,
Filled with laughter that aims to please.
We paint the sky with hopes so bold,
In this utopia, our tales unfold.

Each sharp pencil makes a point,
On paper, we wield our Amigo's joint.
A dome of wonder, a circus bright,
Where every thought ignites delight.

## **Glimpses Beyond Today**

Peeking through the curtains of time,
We spy the future—it's pure crime!
With sneak-a-peeks and hopping sights,
Tomorrow's giggles spark our flights.

In cracked mirrors of yesterday's bluff,
We see reflections that aren't quite tough.
Silly faces and playful grins,
Wrapped in joy, that's how it begins.

Time plays tricks like a playful cat,
Chasing shadows while we sit fat.
Yet in this swirl of wacky spins,
We cheer for laughter as the day begins.

Glances ahead, what fun we'll brew,
With zany antics and skies so blue.
Today may stumble on silly ground,
But when we leap, pure joy is found.

**Wings of Potential**

With wings of laughter, we take flight,
Soaring on dreams through day and night.
Bouncing on clouds of fluffy white,
In our world, wrong is always right.

Tiny thoughts become giant quests,
Silly blunders turn into jest.
Frogs wear crowns and fish can sing,
In this realm, imagination's king.

Flighty ideas dart to and fro,
As we chase giggles down below.
Slipping on rainbows, tripping on rhyme,
Every misstep is just divine.

## Uplifted By Tomorrow's Breeze

A gusty puff, it lifts my hat,
I chase it down, though I'm quite fat.
The clouds above they giggle low,
As I trip over a garden hoe.

The sun peeks out, gives me a wink,
I grab a snack, then spill my drink.
A squirrel dances on the tree,
Laughing at my clumsiness, oh me!

With every breeze, I feel so light,
The bees buzz by with all their might.
They chuckle soft, their wings a blur,
While I just hope my pants won't spur.

In windy games, we laugh and glide,
I follow whims, become the guide.
With every gust, a new surprise,
Tomorrow's fun within the skies.

## The Expansive Canopy

Under a shade where shadows play,
    I find my brain in disarray.
A hammock swings, I dare to dream,
But first, a sandwich—what a theme!

The leaves above start tickling me,
I kick my feet, from branch to tree.
    A lazy cat joins in the fun,
    And like a star, we bask in sun.

The branches dance, they sway and bend,
  They poke my head — it's quite a trend.
So much for peace, I start to shout,
A squirrel chimes in, "What's this about?"

    We laugh together, nature's crew,
In this embrace, the world feels new.
Tomorrow's fun hangs in the air,
As I munch snacks without a care.

## **Mosaic of Bright Horizons**

Colors clash, a painter's dream,
Splashes of joy, laughter's theme.
I trip on paint, it flies around,
Creating art without a sound.

Pinks and yellows, bright as day,
They blend and swirl in funny ways.
A dog trots by, he joins the mess,
Coated in color, he's a success!

With every brush, I paint my fate,
But someone takes my snack plate!
The canvas laughs, shrugs at the theft,
Tomorrow's mischief feels well-kept.

In this mosaic, smiles abound,
Dreams and giggles all around.
We create chaos, joyful pair,
In this colorful world, without a care.

## Flying Towards the Unknown

A kite takes off, so wild and free,
I almost lose my shoe, you see.
It twirls and dips, then gives a shout,
I reel it back—what's this about?

The wind howls loud like a playful pup,
Trying to cheer me—up and up!
With patterns bright, it dances high,
While I stand grounded, wondering why.

A thrill of flight curls in my toes,
My heart beats fast, but nobody knows.
What mischief waits beyond the sky?
My kite might take me—oh my, oh my!

To unknown realms where laughter sings,
Where every breeze brings wacky things.
With each gust, my dreams will soar,
Embracing fun forevermore.

## When Tomorrow Rains Down

When clouds roll in with a belly full of beans,
We'll wear our hats like kings and queens.
Jumping puddles like we're in a dance,
Splashing mud with each chance.

A boat made of paper, we float away,
Sailing on dreams till the end of the day.
Umbrellas turned inside-out, what a sight,
Laughing at thunder, we embrace the fright.

## **Skylit Pathways**

Under the stars on a chocolate bar road,
With giggles and wiggles, we lighten the load.
Each streetlamp a lighthouse, guiding our jest,
And candy-floss clouds at their sugary best.

We strut like peacocks with shoes made of cheese,
Serenading the moon in the soft evening breeze.
With each step we take, we skip and we twirl,
Inventing new dances, we're ready to whirl.

## The Architecture of Hope

Building castles with dreams made of air,
Where giggles and whispers float everywhere.
Pillars of laughter hold up the scene,
In halls made of sunshine, we reign like a queen.

With windows of glass that reflect silly grins,
And roofs made of wishes, our journey begins.
Foundations of friendship laid strong and wide,
In this house of delight, come join for the ride.

## Ascend to the Infinite

Step right up, it's a staircase of fun,
With each funny step, we're practically spun.
Climbing past clouds and tickled skies,
Where laughter is currency, oh what a prize!

We'll wear socks of rainbows and hats with a twist,
As we leap to the stars, can you even resist?
Each rung we conquer, we shout with glee,
Ascending to heights where we just might flee.

## Visions in the Wind

Balloons float high, with a grin so wide,
Chasing a dream on a whimsical ride.
Socks mismatched, a sight to behold,
We dance with the breeze, as stories unfold.

A cat in a hat, perched on a kite,
Sipping on sunshine, oh what a sight!
With giggles of children, laughter takes flight,
In this world of wonder, everything feels right.

## A Tapestry of Tomorrow

Patchwork of futures, each square full of glee,
A toaster that toasts with a wink, just for me!
Jellybeans rain from a sky made of cheer,
We dodge them with joy, let's toast with a beer!

Silly hats bouncing on heads made of fluff,
Every stumble and trip is just part of the fun.
With unicorns prancing in sync to the beat,
We weave through the day, oh, life is a treat.

## Climbing Beyond the Clouds

Ladders of laughter, reaching up high,
Kite strings tugging at the rolling sky.
We hop on a cloud, made of cotton and cream,
And giggle our way through a shimmering dream.

Pancakes for dinner? Oh yes, what a plan!
Dancing with shadows, just me and the can!
With jellyfish swimming in electric blue seas,
Adventure awaits on the soft breezy keys.

## The Light Beyond the Twilight

Fireflies buzzing, a twinkle parade,
Marshmallow sails in the twilight cascade.
With jokes and with jests, we light up the night,
Sipping on starlight, it feels so right.

Sneakers untied, we trip as we race,
Chasing the chuckles that time can't erase.
In a world painted bright with laughter we play,
Who knew tomorrows could be this cliché?

## **Radiance of the Future**

We wear sunglasses at dawn, it's quite absurd,
While squirrels plan this wild new world.
A disco ball hangs from every tree,
As bees learn to dance with glee.

Toasters toast with extra flair,
Pancakes flip without a care.
The stars are plotting a surprise,
With moonlit pies in endless skies.

The future's bright, we just can't see,
Our hats are stuck in a time spree.
Marching along, our shoes will squeak,
As laughter plays the tune we seek.

So let's embrace this zany ride,
With rollercoaster dreams inside.
Each step a giggle, each laugh a cheer,
In this wild world, there's nothing to fear.

## **Blueprints of the Unseen**

The plans were drawn with crayons bright,
A rocket ship made from apple pie.
Elevators stretch to the sky,
While penguins claim the office, oh my!

Blueprints covered in jelly stains,
Architects wearing silly chains.
Mars is now in our backyard,
As dogs bark tunes that hit the card.

The unseen world beams with cheer,
While squirrels build homes with their beer.
Cats wear ties for interviews,
And toast our dreams with giant brews.

Each corner spins with wacky flair,
As buildings dance without a care.
On cookbooks, we write our hopes,
In kitchens filled with jumping slopes.

## **Altitudes of Change**

Upwards we soar on feathered planes,
With rubber duckies in the reins.
Clouds giggle as they float on by,
While pizzas drift in blue sky high.

Kites made from old socks take flight,
Catch the breeze, what a silly sight!
Each gust a joke, a playful tease,
As butterflies plot their launch with ease.

Change is here, with a twist and a spin,
We wear helmets shaped like a fin.
Every fall is a trampoline leap,
In a world where whimsy never sleeps.

So let's bounce up to lofty sights,
With popcorn clouds and sparkling lights.
The altitude's high, but spirits are higher,
In this land, dreams never tire.

## **Boundless Aspirations Above**

Up we go on marshmallow dreams,
With candy bars bursting at the seams.
Kites painted bright with laughter's hue,
While giraffes juggle, just for you.

The sky is a canvas, wild and free,
Filled with wishes of jubilee.
Elevators run on silly juice,
As ducks play chess with a friendly moose.

Every moment bursts with cheer,
As wacky maps draw us near.
Treetops are launching zany quests,
In this world, we are all guests.

So let's leap high, with joy and grace,
In this childlike, wondrous space.
Boundless dreams await their flight,
As we dance amongst the stars tonight.

# A Canopy of Hopes

Underneath this quirky sky,
Cats wear hats and birds all sigh.
Balloons dance high, they seem to twirl,
While squirrels plot to steal the world.

Dreams tumble down like leaves in fall,
Laughter echoes, a playful call.
The sun peeks in, a cheeky grin,
As rainbow sprinkles rain from thin.

Jellybeans fall from clouds above,
While unicorns prance, full of love.
In this space, we chase our fate,
With giggles loud, we celebrate.

So raise your cup, let's toast and cheer,
For whims and wishes drawing near.
With hope as bright as stars that gleam,
We'll find our way and live the dream.

**Tomorrow's Canvas**

The sky's a canvas painted bright,
With stardust dreams that take to flight.
Polka-dotted clouds drift and sway,
As we paint smiles on a rainy day.

A playful splash of color here,
Freckled skies that bring us cheer.
A giant cupcake circles round,
While jellybeans rain on the ground.

Brush strokes of whimsy set the tone,
With candy-coated skies of our own.
Laughter splatters in every hue,
As dreams collide, and then renew.

Let's twist the clouds into funny shapes,
And build our worlds with silly tapes.
Each stroke a giggle, each color a grin,
In this fun dreamscape, we all win!

## Skyward Aspirations

With distant dreams on ladders tall,
We reach for stars and then we fall.
Up goes a kite, catching the breeze,
While ants dance tango beneath the trees.

Bubble gum clouds float past in pairs,
While frogs in tuxedos do their flares.
Ticklish winds tickle our toes,
As we gather dreams like just-washed clothes.

A wobbly rocket makes a flight,
With giggles trailing in pure delight.
Silly wishes on comets soar,
As we laugh and dream—oh, what a score!

So let your heart grow wings and rise,
In this wild world, we touch the skies.
With aspirations wrapped in fun,
We'll chase tomorrow, one by one.

## Celestial Visions Unfurled

Stars tumble down like candy bars,
While fish wear boots and juggle cars.
The moon's a cheese that smells divine,
As we dance under this wobbly line.

Planets play hopscotch in the dark,
Where wishes make a tiny spark.
A giggle here, a chuckle there,
As we ride comets, light as air.

Constellations twirl and spin,
Winking at us with a cheeky grin.
Poking fun at gravity's clutch,
As we leap and twirl—oh, what a touch!

So let's unfurl those dreams galore,
With laughter spilling, we'll explore.
In this celestial dance of delight,
Every vision shines, oh, what a sight!

## Firmament of New Dreams

In a world where cats can fly,
And pigs make coffee from the sky,
We'll toast to all our wild wishes,
With salad bars filled with fishes.

The moon wears socks, a colorful thing,
While turtles pretend it's a spring fling,
We'll dance on clouds, skip and hop,
Where muffins grow at every stop.

Stars throw parties, they twinkle and shine,
They serve us tacos and loads of wine,
Giraffes wear hats, quite out of style,
As we giggle and giggle, for a while.

So join this madcap, whimsical quest,
Where every wrong turn feels like the best,
We'll ride on rainbows, not a care in sight,
In this circus of dreams, oh what a delight!

## Touching the Edge of Tomorrow

Tomorrow waits with its silly grin,
Wearing mismatched socks, can't help but spin,
It juggles time like a seasoned clown,
As we leap into life, never wear a frown.

Flying turtles over candy seas,
Whistling tunes with the buzzing bees,
Join the parade on a bicycle made,
Of chocolate and sprinkles, oh what a trade!

The sun flips pancakes from high above,
While squirrels dance with a shout of love,
It's a festival where all rules bend,
And laughter is the main trend.

So let's run circles, skip and twirl,
Catch the giggles, let laughter swirl,
In this wacky escapade, we feel alive,
In the land of tomorrows, where dreams thrive!

## A Rise into Light

Upward we go, on balloons so bright,
Through frosted donuts, pure delight,
The sun plays hide and seek with the moon,
As we dance to the world's zany tune.

Kites made of cheese float freely by,
While frogs lead us with their sly high-five,
Every giggle hangs like dew on leaves,
In this land where silliness weaves.

With umbrellas made of muffin tops,
We skip through puddles, not caring when we flop,
We'll race with shadows, hand in hand,
In this foolish, merry wonderland.

So raise your cup of jelly beans high,
Toast to the skies and to laughter's supply,
With each step we rise, gleaming with glee,
In this flight of fancy, forever carefree!

## Under the Infinite Dome

Under a dome, quite vast and round,
A cat in a hat just jumped and frowned.
With pancakes flipping, they took flight,
Landing softly, what a sight!

A dog in socks joins the party too,
Wearing sunglasses, oh what a view!
Chasing shadows of flying pies,
Giggles erupt, oh how time flies!

A bird on a bicycle zooms through the air,
Wobbling wildly without a care.
With feathers fluffed and a grin so wide,
Who knew fun could be this bizarre ride?

Beneath this dome, all worries cease,
In this moment, we find our peace.
Laughter echoes, a joyful tune,
Living life under the playful moon.

## **Beyond the Sunlit Veil**

Beyond the veil, where ducks wear ties,
Laughter echoes in endless skies.
A squirrel juggles acorns with glee,
Claiming the title: King of Quirk, you see!

A rabbit roller-skates, what a show!
While the sunflowers cheer, stealing the glow.
They dance in a circle, a silly parade,
With confetti of petals, never dismayed!

A fish in a top hat recites a rhyme,
Claiming, 'I'm late!' for a meeting at prime.
As clouds above burst with giggles and grace,
This whimsical world is a lively embrace!

With each silly twist, new joys emerge,
A kaleidoscope of laughter does surge.
Through the veil, where fun reigns supreme,
Life's a wacky and wonderful dream!

## **Future Raindrops**

Raindrops in colors, oh so bright,
Fall on umbrellas in pure delight.
Dancing on rooftops with joyous glee,
Each drop a giggle, wild and free!

They're not just water, but jellybeans too,
Splashes of fun, in a sky so blue.
Puddles reflect through a quirky lens,
Jumping in rain—who needs dry ends?

Bouncing raindrops play hopscotch on snails,
While giggling worms tell silly tales.
With umbrellas twirling, they form a choir,
Singing the songs of a cheerful shire!

Droplets whisper secrets, oh what a thrill,
As laughter and joy flow down the hill.
In this future, where smiles take flight,
Each rain-soaked moment feels just right!

## Echoes of Tomorrow's Light

In echoes of light, the bunnies race,
Chasing rainbows, oh what a pace!
With shoes made of marshmallows, soft and sweet,
They bounce and tumble, quick on their feet!

A dapper penguin flaunts his new hat,
Waddling along with a well-dressed cat.
They share a toast with fizzy delight,
Champagne made of berries, a fabulous sight!

Twinkling stars join in the fun,
Performing a ballet, a dazzling run.
With giggles and chuckles, they shine so bright,
In the echoing laughter of tomorrow's light!

A grand celebration of whims and cheer,
Where nothing is dull, and joy is near.
In this space of humor and bliss,
Every moment's a treasure, none to miss!

## Beneath the Shadow of Progress

Underneath great beams of steel,
We dance in shoes with wheels.
Construction hats are all the rage,
As we scribble dreams upon the stage.

With blueprints drawn on napkins wide,
The architects must laugh and hide.
For every plan that hits the ground,
A rubber chicken might be found.

Materials stacked in quite a mess,
We're building worlds, oh what a stress!
But in this chaos, joy we find,
A trampoline to make us blind.

So sip your coffee, make it grand,
While juggling bricks with a steady hand.
Progress may have its clumsy days,
But we're here, with silly ways.

## A Visionary Umbra

In shadows cast by wild ideas,
We sketch our plans with giggling cheers.
Umbrellas turned inside out in flight,
Creating storms in the fading light.

The future calls from cloudy roofs,
Where laughter echoes and logic goofs.
We'll bounce our thoughts off walls so high,
While wearing hats that look awry.

With espresso shots in paper cups,
We'll build a spaceship using just pups.
Gorillas dance upon our heads,
As pigeons plot their lofty spreads.

To dream in colors bold and bright,
While painting rainbows in the night.
So let's embrace this funny fate,
And laugh at all we create.

## Horizon of Dreams

On distant shores, we plant our flags,
As seagulls swoop with humble gags.
With surfboards crafted from old spoons,
We ride the waves of crinkled tunes.

Kites fly high with socks on string,
While silly songs create a ring.
Today's mistakes become our gems,
A pirate crew with whimsy stems.

The sun may rise and set anew,
But we'll adorn it with a shoe!
With every quirk, our spirits dream,
As laughter dances in the beam.

So gather 'round, let shenanigans flow,
For what is life without the show?
In every skip and every gleam,
We find a way to steer our dream.

## **Whispering Skies Above**

Up above where giggles soar,
The clouds are fluffed, we yearn for more.
With cotton candy on our heads,
We skip 'round fields of rainbow beds.

Balloons inflated with silly thoughts,
Chase after cats in polka dots.
A kite caught up in laughter's trance,
Dancers twirl in a goofy dance.

While rainstorms play the tambourine,
We jump through puddles, like it's a scene.
Each drop a note in a funny tune,
As shadows prance beneath the moon.

So let us toast with soda streams,
To all the wacky, wild dreams!
In skies so bright, we'll laugh and sing,
For silly times are the real king.

## **Starlit Dreams in Disguise**

In hats of tin, we gaze at stars,
Upon our dreams, we travel far.
With moonlit beams, we'll plan our flights,
Like squirrels with plans on sleepless nights.

We sketch out views from rooftops high,
In goofy goggles, we aim for the sky.
Our hopes take shape like bread in dough,
As laughter spills, the magic grows.

A trampoline bounces our thoughts afloat,
On paper boats, we'll steer our quote.
With giggles loud, we'll build a fleet,
Of dreams that dance on our own two feet.

So here we stand, in joy we bask,
With silly hats, no need to ask.
The stars are close, our joy sublime,
As we craft futures one joke at a time.

## The Future's Skyward Veil

With straws and tape, we build our dreams,
In fanciful hats, we plot our schemes.
A cloud of hopes, we wear with flair,
While rubber chickens float in the air.

Our blueprint's made of jelly beans,
As giggles burst in vibrant themes.
We leap through space, like kangaroos,
Crafting bright paths, we sing our blues.

In bubble wrap, our voices soar,
As wishes dance on the candy floor.
We paint our futures in colors wild,
Like giggling kids, forever beguiled.

So let's ascend with glee and cheer,
In this wacky world, there's nothing to fear.
With veggie crowns and laughter bright,
We'll chase tomorrow into the night.

## Architectural Aspirations

With pizza boxes stacked so high,
We dream of towers that scrape the sky.
Our plans are drawn with crayons bold,
In a kingdom where fun never gets old.

We throw around ideas like confetti,
With sleepy squirrels and woes that are petty.
Our dreams are vast, like a cereal bowl,
Crafting skyscrapers with an oatmeal soul.

With giggles and glue, we'll pave the way,
To a neighborhood where we all can play.
A castle made of candy, a moat of cream,
Like marshmallow clouds, we float on a dream.

So join our crew, let's build and frolic,
In dreams of light and a fun symbolic.
As we brainstorm under a feathered plume,
Together we'll dance in architectural bloom.

## **Whispers of Celestial Designs**

We scribble notes on the backs of cats,
In hats of cheese, we're dream architects.
With moonbeam pencils, we draft our cheer,
As candy sprinkles light up the sphere.

Our plans take flight on bubblegum wings,
In a land of marshmallows, where laughter rings.
We sketch out worlds with giggles and glee,
Like fireflies lighting our destiny.

We spin in circles, with dreams so grand,
A chocolate fountain, a jellybean land.
With whispers soft, our visions unite,
As we build our hopes, sparkling and bright.

So come along, wear your silliest grin,
In this playful realm, together we win.
Tomorrow's glow is a funny surprise,
As we dance with joy, chasing the skies.

## Skylines of Hope

Up high where dreams do bounce,
Squirrels in suits, they prance and pounce.
Pigeons with ties, they flit around,
In the city's joy, new quirks abound.

Clouds wear shades, they grin and tease,
As laughter dances on the breeze.
Ladders seem to lead up high,
To places where the pizza flies.

Giraffes on rooftops, sipping tea,
Debating if life's just a spree.
Skyscrapers wave, they twist and shout,
While silly goats wander about.

In this playful place up above,
Joy springs forth like a dove.
A skyline painted in jolly hues,
Where wishes waltz and dreams amuse.

## Vistas of Change

Bunnies bake pies in the evening glow,
Wearing hats that steal the show.
Sunlight pours like syrup sweet,
While dancing ants tap to a beat.

Kites soar high, defying laws,
As a cat conducts with a paw!
Rainbows slide down silver beams,
In a land adorned with dreams.

Clocks tick-tock with a funny face,
Transforming time in a breezy race.
Old trees wiggle, shedding bark,
As giggles echo in the park.

What wonders lie just out of view,
In every shade, a chance anew.
With each whisper of change so bright,
Laughter rides the wings of light.

## Horizons of Possibility

A snail in a car zooms down the way,
Wearing a cap that's quite the display.
Fish on bicycles flounder and glide,
As a turtle takes them for a ride.

Gates to worlds where llamas sing,
And every day brings a new fling.
Zebras in pajamas, oh what a sight,
Dancing in stripes under starry night.

Mountains chuckle, "Oh, we can't wait,
To see where all this fun will skate."
Balloons in trees wear hats like kings,
In a realm where anything springs.

With each step, new paths unwind,
Funny faces in the living kind.
Frogs toast to dreams stretching far and wide,
In this paradise where joy won't hide.

## Embracing the New Dawn

Roosters wear shades at break of day,
Strutting around in a bright array.
Sunshine tickles the sleepy roofs,
As cats juggle muffins, defending their hooves.

Coffee streams in a purple cup,
While rabbits hop, never giving up.
Socks mix colors like a wild bouquet,
In this fresh start, come what may.

The sunrise winks, "Let's paint the skies,"
With laughter, sparkles, and silly sighs.
Every morning brings a fresh new jest,
In this funfair, we're truly blessed.

So raise your mugs, let's cheer and sing,
For each turn brings the best of spring.
Chasing horizons, we'll never frown,
In the land where laughter wears the crown.

## **Celestial Hopes**

Stars are giggling in the night,
Balloons on strings, oh what a sight.
A monkey swings with dreams so big,
Dancing atop, wearing a wig.

Clouds will whisper jokes so sly,
While rainbows wink as they glide by.
Wish upon a cheeky star,
And laugh until we reach so far.

## **The Height of Possibility**

Kites are tangled in the breeze,
Tickling tops of wobbly trees.
Up they go, in silly flairs,
Chasing squirrels with acrobats' glares.

Giraffes in shades, they take a stand,
With ice cream cones in each long hand.
Reaching high, they may just fall,
But laughter rings, the best of all!

## Skyward Journeys

Penguins in planes, oh what a ride,
Flipping pancakes as they glide.
Pigeons singing pop songs loud,
A feathered crew, they feel so proud.

Chasing dreams on feathered wings,
Surprising joy as laughter rings.
With every turn, they twist and sway,
Through cotton candy clouds they play.

## A Canvas of New Beginnings

Brushes dipped in bright delight,
Painting laughter in the light.
Silly hats and wobbly shoes,
Artistic moments we can't refuse.

Splat! A blob of joyful glee,
Smiles abound, it's clear to see.
Every stroke and silly grin,
A masterpiece where fun begins!

## Chasing the Ethereal Horizon

Up here where the pigeons plot,
We're kings of a paper boat.
With dreams as hats and clouds as shoes,
We dance on beams made of pure prose.

Windswept hair and laughter loud,
We argue with the wispy cloud.
Bouncing thoughts like rubber balls,
We scribble jokes on cedar walls.

The sun's a cheeky, golden grin,
While gravity forgets to spin.
We swing from stars, we're childlike charms,
As moonbeams tickle with gentle arms.

So take a leap, come fly with me,
Where skies are bright and hearts are free.
For up above, where dreams collide,
We'll find the joy that we can't hide.

## Untouched Heights of Tomorrow

In a world where balloons won't pop,
We juggle rainbows, watch them drop.
With marshmallow clouds beneath our feet,
We skip like stones to our own beat.

Chasing rockets shaped like fish,
We count the stars, and make a wish.
On unmade beds of cotton candy,
We giggle loud, feeling quite dandy.

The sky's a playground, swings worldwide,
Each cloud a friend, go for a ride.
We sculpt our dreams in every hue,
As laughter echoes, old turns new.

In untouched heights, we laugh and play,
Where whimsy leads, let's find our way.
So gather round, let's take a seat,
On the marshmallow clouds, life is sweet.

## **Cloudbound Reveries**

A wobbly step on a sugar high,
With giggles flying, oh my oh my!
The clouds roll in like fluffy dreams,
As we choreograph silly schemes.

Balancing wishes on a beam,
We tuck in laughter, or so it seems.
With starry eyes and jigsaw minds,
We piece together what life finds.

Airships made of giggles and wraps,
Chasing shadows in silly naps.
The sky's a canvas, paint it bright,
With colors sprouting in moonlight.

In reveries where whimsy reigns,
We dance the clouds, forget the trains.
Just float along, don't miss the show,
For in our hearts, the joy will grow.

## **Skylines of the Unseen**

Beneath a sky sewn with twinkling threads,
We pounce on rainbows gossiping in reds.
With capes of laughter and boots of glee,
We soar through jokes, wild and free.

In the skyline where echoes prance,
We spin our tales, give them a chance.
With clouds that tease and giggle anew,
The world's a stage, just me and you.

Each star a wink, a playful nudge,
We tackle gravity, we won't budge.
In this circus of dreams, we take the stage,
With open hearts, we'll turn the page.

So let's weave dreams on a silver thread,
In unseen skylines where none should tread.
With humor bright, we'll light the night,
And dance amidst laughter, pure delight.

## The Promise Above

A ceiling of dreams, quite askew,
With laundry flapping, quite the view.
Each sock a promise, a hope to soar,
Giggles abound, who knows what's in store?

Dancing among clouds, all dressed in white,
A kite caught a laugh, it took off in flight.
With whispers of plans and a wink of a star,
We'll make our own rules, no matter how far.

Up here, every bump becomes a great jest,
Where shadows do tango, we feel so blessed.
Wobbly ambitions, a merry parade,
In this rooftop circus, we're never afraid.

So come join the fun beneath our wide grin,
With each twist and turn, let the laughter begin.
For the promise above is a joke we all share,
A whimsical venture, floating high in the air.

## **Futures Adrift on the Breeze**

Balloons full of dreams float past with delight,
Each twist and turn spins a tale in the light.
With popcorn clouds, we laugh all the way,
As futures adrift choose their own quirky play.

Whispers of change ride the gusty old zephyrs,
Tickling our fancies, like forgotten treasures.
A teacup sails by, with a grin on its face,
Promising journeys at a comical pace.

Tick tock on the breeze, time wears silly shoes,
With every gust bending pathways we choose.
This carousel of fate spins faster than thought,
Welcome to tomorrow, oh what have we brought?

Gales of laughter lift spirits on high,
As dreams turn to sillies, drifting by in the sky.
So grab hold of joy, as we play our own roles,
On futures adrift, with lighthearted souls.

## Touched by the Winds of Change

The winds of change blow, tickling our toes,
Whirling in chaos, where anything goes.
A hat takes flight, what a marvelous sight,
As we chase after dreams, with giggles and might.

Each whisper of fate carries tales of delight,
Balloon animals giggle, dancing in sight.
With sprinkles of whimsy and laughter so bright,
The world's a big joke, let's laugh through the night.

As kites tease the clouds with their colorful glee,
Unruly ambitions flutter wild and free.
Change is a jester, prancing with flair,
Wearing mismatched socks, with no single care.

So raise up your glasses, let's toast to the breeze,
For life's a grand circus, with tricks done with ease.
In the charm of the winds, we find joy in the strange,
We're all in this comedy, touched by the change.

## Celestial Canopies

Beneath a sky painted with jellybean hues,
Celestial canopies hide whimsical views.
Stars wear their sunglasses, sunbathing up high,
As moonbeams tickle us from way up in the sky.

A comet bursts forth with confetti and flair,
Making our wishes dance in midair.
With each twinkling laugh of the cosmos above,
We float on clouds, wrapped in giggles of love.

Galactic giggles endearingly spin,
While planets do dances, inviting us in.
With every strange orbit, we cheer and we grin,
For joy is the ticket to every wild win.

So join our crusade, let whimsy take flight,
In celestial canopies, everything's right.
As laughs echo softly through infinite space,
Life's simply a joke, let's savor the grace.

## **Sanctuary of Starlit Dreams**

Underneath the cosmic glow,
We built a fort of pillows low,
Squirrels laugh, and cats conspire,
To reach the moon, we'll need a wire.

Our snacks are stardust, brewed with care,
We wear our hats, a fancy fare,
The stars, they twinkle—what a tease!
Do they know how to ride the breeze?

He said, 'A comet just went by!'
I tripped, but still I swear to fly,
With every misstep, laughter blooms,
As dreams escape our cozy rooms.

In this sanctuary of delight,
We'll chase the sun 'til late at night,
And when the dawn begins to glow,
We'll nap and dream of skies aglow.

## The Ascent of Ambition

Climbing stairs made of marshmallows,
Each step creaks, a sound that mellows,
With goals as lofty as my snacks,
I plan to conquer—wait, what's that flack?

A ladder made of licorice,
I reach for dreams and share a wish,
Oops! I slipped, I'm flying high,
I'll land in a cake, oh my, oh my!

Ambition sways like jellybeans,
I'll scale the peaks of candy dreams,
With every slip, a giggled cheer,
Success is sweet when friends are near.

So up we go, with laughter loud,
Our dreams are bold, we're feeling proud,
We'll reach the clouds, and then we'll play,
In this silly, sweet ballet.

## Kaleidoscope of Tomorrow

Through a prism of silly sights,
We see the world in quirky lights,
With every twist, a new embrace,
Oh look, my dog's just lost his face!

Colors mingle, shapes collide,
The dance of dreams, we should abide,
Penguins wear hats, and cats may sing,
A chorus of joy in everything.

Tomorrow's just a dance away,
With sliding shoes and a foggy sway,
Laughter bursting like confetti,
We float through time—oh isn't it petty?

In this kaleidoscope so bright,
We'll turn the wrongs to silly rights,
And as we spin, we'll laugh and twirl,
In our darling, wacky world.

## Dreams Beneath the Celestial

Beneath the twinkles, dreams do fuse,
A nightly game of 'who will snooze?'
The sky giggles with stars so spry,
While owls compete in a sleepy sigh.

With marshmallow clouds, we softly drift,
Chasing giggles, we play and lift,
In this haven, laughter reigns,
As unicorns tease the poppy trains.

The comet's tail is made of cream,
It melts away, a silly dream,
Yet here we lie, our spirits bold,
With joy and whimsy, we'll never fold.

So we dream on, beneath the night,
With every laugh, our hearts take flight,
In the celestial tune we hear,
Fun is the song, let's persevere!

## Guardians of the Skyline

Up high with capes and flair,
We keep watch from thin air.
With sandwiches and a drink,
We laugh as we start to think.

Birds are jealous of our view,
As we plot the grand to do.
A tower made of jelly beans,
Who knew that was in our genes?

## Skylines in the Making

Building dreams with silly tools,
Measuring with rulers—who needs rules?
A giant slide from floor to floor,
Watch us glide, we shout for more!

Cement boots for that added flair,
Dancing on beams—oh, we don't care!
We balance and teeter, what a ride,
As our wild plans take the sky wide!

## The Canopy of Innovation

Underneath our leafy scheme,
Life's a bright and zany dream.
We use recycled socks to build,
A fortress fair, oh so thrilled!

With every duct tape cross we make,
We giggle at the things that shake.
Inventing laughter as we try,
To float our ideas into the sky!

## **Shadows of Altitude**

In the shadows, we take a leap,
Making clouds from silly sheep.
We giggle as we grab the air,
Pretending we have not a care!

Hats made of foil to catch the light,
Invisible strings pulling us right.
We chase the dreams that float so high,
While sipping juice, oh my, oh my!

## Ascent to New Heights

Up we go, on a ladder so high,
With a cat in a hat that just won't comply.
He wears a grin and keeps sliding down,
While I shake my fist at this ludicrous clown.

The clouds are our neighbors, they wave from afar,
They dive and they zoom in a cloud-shaped car.
With snacks made of stardust, we feast like the pros,
But someone forgot the ketchup, goodness knows!

Our trampoline's made of dreams and of laughs,
Where we bounce into giggles, not fearing the gaffs.
The spring in our step, quite literally grand,
We leap over rainbows, light as a band.

With every ascent, potential is found,
A penguin in shorts keeps us spinning around.
We dance with the breezes, all silly and bright,
As we tickle the skies, it's a ridiculous sight.

## **Dreamscapes Above**

Floating on marshmallows, a fluffy delight,
We ride on a dragon who thinks he's polite.
He'll drop us in puddles of jelly-filled cheer,
As we giggle and wiggle, there's nothing to fear.

Chasing our shadows on bikes made of twine,
We whip up the weather like it's fresh sweet wine.
Lightning bugs join in, forming a crew,
With disco ball skies, we dance on the dew.

Our friends are all dancing in pajamas of stars,
While munching on moonbeams and shiny candy bars.
We play hopscotch with time, counting stars in between,
Jumping right into dreams with a hop and a glean.

At dusk, we paint rainbows, in colors so wild,
With crayons made of giggles, laugh lines compiled.
We sketch out dimensions where silliness reigns,
In dreamscapes above, we escape the mundane.

## **Tapestry of Futures**

We weave our adventures with threads made of fun,
Stitching fast our stories under the sun.
With every big knot, a mishap we see,
The fabric of whimsy embraces you and me.

The loom's an accordion, it plays a fine tune,
While we dance on the edges of a glorious moon.
Each thread is a giggle, each patch is a grin,
In this wacky creation, we always win.

Sailing on paper boats that giggle and sway,
We find treasure maps that lead us astray.
The compass is broken, but maps never lie,
As long as we're laughing, we'll just fly high.

In this tapestry bright, we're all interlaced,
A patchwork of futures, together we faced.
So spin me a tale where the moon wears a hat,
And let's thread our joy in a place that's all chat.

## Twilight of Possibilities

As the sun takes a bow, and the stars start to play,
We giggle at shadows that dance in the fray.
The light bulbs are winking, they know what's in store,
In this whimsical twilight, we yearn for much more.

We climb up the starlight, we smear it on toast,
With jam made of laughter, we'll give it a boast.
Each bite's like a giggle, a burst of delight,
In this twilight of dreams, we soar through the night.

With loony balloons, all inflated with cheer,
We float through horizons, horizons so near.
Every moment's a joke wrapped in glee, of a sort,
In this twilight, we jest, it's our own little sport.

The future is funny, a riddle of types,
With slapstick adventures, and giggles in stripes.
So gather your friends for a joyful discourse,
Under twinkling tongues, we'll ride that wild horse.

## **Skyward Visions**

Up high where dreams take flight,
Squirrels play with clouds at night.
Birds wear hats, and they all dance,
Daring each other for a chance.

Sunbeams bounce like rubber balls,
Chasing down the raindrop falls.
A kite takes off, it swirls and twirls,
Imitating all the world's girls.

Laughter drifts on gentle zephyrs,
While owls hoot in silly whispers.
Popcorn clouds, let's reach for more,
In a land of skies to explore.

## Beneath Tomorrow's Canopy

Underneath this leafy charm,
Llamas knit with utmost calm.
Giraffes juggle sweet, ripe pears,
While hippos gossip without cares.

Sunlight sprinkles lemonade,
As dancing ants make a parade.
Bumblebees wear tiny shades,
Making sure their style never fades.

With each breeze, we taste the fun,
It's never dull; it's just begun.
Join the party under green,
Where the laughter's always seen.

**Horizons Unbound**

Far away, where giggles fly,
Pigs take selfies in the sky.
Elephants balancing on a ball,
Let's see who can't help but fall!

Banana boats on a cotton sea,
Chasing dreams so wild and free.
Fish in tuxedos, what a sight!
They twirl and swirl with pure delight.

Every star, a jokes' retake,
Winking down, it loves to bake.
Join the fun; don't you wait,
Tomorrow's here—it's really great!

## Above the Urban Symphony

Up above the city's din,
Rats in tuxes start to spin.
Rooftop parties with cake galore,
Dancing while the taxis roar.

Pigeons croon old pop songs loud,
While we twirl amongst the crowd.
Balloons float like dreams in tow,
As rainbows paint the skyline's flow.

A saxophone plays jazzy tunes,
Joined by crickets, and some raccoons.
City life, a wacky frame,
Beneath the laughter, nothing's tame.

## **The Horizon Beckons**

A trampoline tucked in the sky,
With clouds as our comfy bed,
We bounce to the edge, oh so spry,
While rain douses dreams in blue dread.

We surf on beams of golden light,
And giggle as stars make a fuss,
What if comets start a pillow fight?
Never mind, just hop on the bus!

The sun wears shades to look cool,
While moonbeams throw a raucous fair,
We dance like kids skipping school,
Waving our silliness in the air!

Let's climb to the peak with a snack,
Popcorn stashed in our cosmic view,
We'll laugh at gravity's sneaky knack,
And find sweet giggles in the blue!

## Celestial Pathways

Shooting stars lace the evening sky,
With giggles that echo like chimes,
We follow the trail with a sly eye,
Finding mischief in cosmic rhymes.

Clouds wearing hats, caught in jest,
We skip over rainbows, oh so spry,
Count heart-shaped clouds as a test,
While squirrels debate, 'Will we fly?'

The sun plays tag, so bright and bold,
While shadows giggle and dance around,
We write our tales in stardust gold,
Chasing the laughter that knows no bound!

With each tickle from a sunbeam's wink,
We gather our dreams like the finest dust,
To float on a breeze, oh don't you think,
This cosmic caper is a must!

## **Infinity Underfoot**

Squishing clouds beneath our feet,
Stomping puddles filled with glee,
Each bounce is a silly beat,
As cosmos laughs, 'Come dance with me!'

We catch whispers from the stars,
Trading jokes with moonlit charms,
Charting paths to Jupiter's bars,
Where aliens serve hot cocoa with arms.

Galactic hops and silly skips,
Make the universe spin and sway,
With every grin, a comet tips,
As we paint the night, in a playful way!

With starry roulades cascading down,
We leap through wonders, light as air,
No frowns allowed in this cosmic town,
Just joy and jests everywhere!

## Cascading Promises

A waterfall of giggles falls,
From mountains made of jellybeans,
We leap between the rainbow calls,
And slip on optimism's sheens.

Each drip is a promise of delight,
With rainbows bouncing through our hair,
Jumping clouds, oh what a sight,
Who knew mischief lived up there?

Silly whispers float like balloons,
We pluck the stars for midnight snacks,
With chocolate rivers under moons,
And laughter chasing after tracks.

Frogs wear crowns in this whimsical place,
Serenade the sun with hop and skip,
Let's vow to keep a silly pace,
And dance our dreams with a lollipop trip!

## **Perches of Tomorrow**

On a ledge of dreams we sit,
Wearing hats that don't quite fit.
We trade our jokes with the breeze,
And laugh at clouds floating with ease.

A squirrel dressed in a tiny coat,
Gives a speech on a distant boat.
The pigeons roll their eyes in glee,
As we debate the best kind of tea.

With slingshots made of rubber bands,
We launch our hopes to distant lands.
Who knew the sky could be so bright?
While we stay up to greet the night.

And when the sun starts to peek,
We're still awake, barely speak.
These perches hold our wildest plans,
In the world where fun begins and spans.

## **Illuminated Futures Above**

Under twinkling stars so bold,
We share our secrets, dreams untold.
A disco ball sways in the wind,
While silly visions just begin.

The moon wears shades, to look so cool,
And dances over our makeshift school.
We teach the owls our finest tunes,
While the crickets play their afternoon.

We toss our future like a frisbee,
Landing tricks that seem so cheesy.
An umbrella opens with a spin,
Catching laughter, where we begin.

With every spark and gleeful shout,
We float amidst the stars, no doubt.
This spot above, our minds take flight,
Illuminated by our laughter's light.

## Rising Above the Ordinary

On rooftops high, we plot our schemes,
With grass-stuffed pillows, living dreams.
A cat wearing glasses plays chess,
While we create our own success.

We use old kites as our umbrellas,
Dancing in patterns like silly fellas.
The clouds roll in like a friendly band,
As we paint rainbows above the land.

Lemonade rivers twist and flow,
With sprinkles that glimmer and glow.
We challenge gravity, soar like birds,
In a world where laughter's the only word.

Let's think of wonders, strange and new,
Climbing higher in a wacky stew.
There's joy in rising so unreal,
Above the ordinary, we spin the wheel.

## Winds of Change

With hats a-flap in the playful gusts,
We shout our dreams, in breezy trusts.
A kite tied to whimsy soars high,
As we steal glances at the sky.

Grandma's pot of soup on the grill,
Steam forms shapes, a mountain thrill.
We slip and slide on banana peels,
While laughing loudly at our deals.

An acorn's plan to grow and spread,
Has us sipping tea, stars over our head.
We ride on gusts, with carefree cheer,
As wind whispers secrets we hold dear.

So grab your jester hat with glee,
The winds of change set our minds free.
In this whirl of fun, we'll embrace,
A silly dance in outer space.

www.ingramcontent.com/pod-product-compliance
Lightning Source LLC
Chambersburg PA
CBHW070008300426
43661CB00141B/371